ORIGIN AND HISTORY

Ancestors of the Chow Chow, according to historians, trace back to the dogs of the Arctic Circle, their descendants having migrated from there into Siberia, Mongolia, and China. By some, the Chow is considered to have been a "basic breed," which is to be found in the heritage of the majority of the Northern Dogs (including the Keeshond, Norwegian Elkhound, Pomeranian, and Samoyed, among others). Those who do not accept this theory insist that the earliest Chow Chows owe their existence to a Samoyed cross with a Mastiff from Tibet—a creditable theory when one considers the facial expression of the Chow. As with the majority of breeds, an exact factual background is difficult to pinpoint, for who can say for certain in what sequence events took place so many centuries ago?

In China, the progenitors of the modern Chow Chow were

This smooth Chow Chow proudly poses next to a statue of a fellow Chinaman—the ancient Foo Dog.

basically the only canines bred for this purpose in that country. Difficult as it may be to picture, we are told that Chow Chows excelled in the roles of both pointers and retrievers during the famous Imperial Hunts, with as many as 2000 of them having been kept by one Chinese Emperor whose force of huntsmen numbered 10,000.

When the great hunts no longer took place, the selective breeding of Chow Chows became, to most people, decreasingly important. However, a small nucleus of fanciers, principally noblemen and the wealthy, did continue to breed Chow Chows on a limited scale—a fact which undoubtedly saved the breed from extinction at the time.

The diversity of Chow capabilities was considerable, which may surprise the modern fancier accustomed to thinking of these handsome animals primarily as companions and pets. Early Chows were used as working dogs as well as for hunting. They had also distinguished themselves as sled dogs, their powerful structure equipping them well for this purpose. The author suspects that, were they to be asked to perform some of these duties in present times, the instinct and heritage of the Chow Chow would efficiently come to life.

with the breed? Another explanation is that the name was coined from the Chinese word "chaou," this referring to a dog of great strength, which would also seem appropriate.

The Chow Chow's most unique distinguishing feature is the blue-black tongue and mouth color. This and the characteristic scowl are the two features of particular significance to the breed. Dogs

R.M. Moore's rendition of Peridot, owned by Lady Granville Gordon and daughter, Lady Faudel Phillips. The black dog in the portrait is Ch. Blue Blood.

The name "Chow Chow" has created many stories, theories, and wide speculation; including the belief that the dogs, upon occasion, were used for food in their native land. The most likely story is that dogs traveling from China to England by clipper ship usually made the trip in the hold, where the assorted objects sharing this space were habitually referred to as "chow chow" and the area all occupied known as the "chow hold." What is more natural then this name sticking

possessing these features were known in England well back into the 19th century.

Chow Chows started to "take off" in popularity when the Earl of Lonsdale, an admirer of the breed, became one of its most distinguished and influential enthusiasts. Throughout his lifetime, this gentleman's love of Chows flourished; the result of his having received one as a gift during one of his frequent trips to the Far East, which he in turn presented to relatives. These were

Lady Faudel Phillips, a great Chowist, with Ch. Pang Tse of Amwell photographed in 1929.

the Marquis and Marchioness of Huntley who, owing to the charms of their puppy, promptly wanted more of these magnificent dogs. Consequently, subsequent trips found the Earl of Lonsdale commissioned to bring additional imports from China to Great Britain for this couple.

It was the Marchionness of Huntley who assembled England's first influential kennel of Chows, dogs whose quality continued through future generations, thus having true influence on the breed. She sold a dog named Peridot to another fancier, Lady Faudel Phillips, and he distinguished himself by becoming Best in Show in 1895 at the famous Ladies Kennel Club Championship Dog Show.

Lady Faudel Phillips was the daughter of another of England's earliest Chow Chow breeders, Lady Granville Gordon. Her

kennel, Amwell, continued until her death in 1943.

The first British-bred Champion Chow was Ch. Blue Blood, (the progeny of red parents but a blue dog himself) who was bred by Lady Granville Gordon.

Queen Victoria added a Chow Chow to her own varied kennel in (or about) 1865—a guarantee that the breed would be popular with British aristocracy.

A black bitch, Chinese Puzzle, was the first Chow to be exhibited at the Crystal Palace Dog Show in London in 1880. Three years later, Chows received their own breed classification for the first time, moving them up from their "foreign dog" classification. And in 1894, the first Chow Chow was accepted for registration in the British Stud Book.

This trophy was presented by The Earl of Lonsdale to the Chinese Chow Club in 1911 and won by Sidonia in 1915. This particular photograph appeared in Lady Faudel Phillips's scrapbook.

In the United States, Chows also were starting to arouse interest and, in June 1905, the first of the breed gained title of "Champion." This was an importation, Chinese Chum, belonging to Mrs. Charles E. Proctor (who owned the Blue Dragon Kennels). Chum's later successes included the winning of Best of Breed at the Westminster Kennel Club in 1906; of still greater note is his role of helping to establish the breed in America by his outstanding ability to sire Chows of outstanding merit. Among his offspring in the United States were Night of Asia, who followed Chum to championship within a few months, and the importantly influential Ch. Black Cloud. As they were descended from England's leading bloodlines, these dogs were successful in reproducing their quality in America, thus contributing well to their breed.

Fifteen years prior to the occasion of Chinese Chum's completed AKC championship, the first recorded Chow in the entry list at an American dog show appeared at the Westminster Kennel Club in

Mrs. Calvin Coolidge and a black Chow Chow, Timmy, photographed in 1929.

1890. He was entered as a Chinese Chow Chow Dog, was named Takya, and belonged to Miss A. C. Derby.

The Chow Chow Club of America is the parent club for the breed and is one of the oldest specialty clubs in the United States. This organization came into being in 1906. Dr. Henry Jarrett, owner of a Chow named Yen How who was an important early winner, served as Club Secretary for the first 35 years of its existence.

Among the earliest Chow Chow kennels of distinction in the United States was Winsum, belonging to Mrs. Franklin Hutton, which had famous dogs in the breed as early as 1911.

Many dedicated breeders and famous dogs have contributed to the development of Chow Chow quality in both England and the United States, the two greatest strongholds of the breed. Those of you who wish to learn more on the subject will find excellent sources of complete Chow Chow knowledge through three books: *The World of the Chow Chow* by

There are many excellent sources of information on the Chow Chow. These three books are published by T.F.H. Publications and are a must in every Chow fancier's library.

Dr. Samuel Draper and Joan Brearley; *The Chow Chow* by Anna Katherine Nicholas, with special chapters by Desmond Murphy; and *The Book of the Chow Chow* also by Dr. Samuel Draper and Joan Brearley. These are available from T.F.H. Publications, and are filled with exciting information regarding the Chow Chow's development in a manner for which space here is insufficient.

Canada is another country where Chow Chows are successful and popular. This is the home of the Bu Dynasty Kennels (owned by Mr. and Mrs. Herb Williams and Fred Peddie), which have produced winners around the world. There are dozens of other kennels breeding Chows of merit, from coast to coast in Canada, where the individuality and charm of the breed are well loved and appreciated.

Europe and South America have many winning Chows, and "down under" in Australia, we find good quality and devoted breeders producing very typical and handsome members of this breed.

LIVING WITH A CHOW CHOW

Chow Chows obviously have a good deal to offer their owners as they bring special pleasure and pride of ownership—a fact made eloquently clear by the impressive gain in American Kennel Club registrations of this breed, which have increased to the point where they rank on the list of the top 20 breeds in the United States.

There are many of us around who can recall that, some 60 years ago, prospective dog fanciers were inclined to regard these dogs with reservation, insofar as ownership was concerned, due to their "sharpness" and lack of steady reliability, which sometimes seemed to hinge a bit on hostility. We feel it is particularly remarkable, therefore, that the pendulum has swung to where the Chow Chow is a dog equally noted for his beauty of appearance and of character.

The success with which this

A Chow Chow puppy has a lot to offer his owner, as he brings a special pleasure and pride of ownership.

has been achieved has been created by good ownership, intelligent relationships, and a great deal of caring on the part of Chow Chow breeders and admirers. Those loving the breed had no intention of permitting it to be forever known as an untrustworthy dog, and they set about the task of assuring that their puppies became loving and lovable, reliable, loyal and well-dispositioned canine citizens.

This achievement has come about through emphasis on socialization, in the raising of and living with Chow Chows. From earliest puppyhood (about one week's age, and prior to the eyes opening), responsible owners of Chow Chow litters start to work on the development of desirable breed personality. The baby Chow Chow learns to love and trust humans from their attitude toward and care of the

Today's Chow Chow is noted for both his beauty of appearance and his nobility of character.

A properly socialized Chow puppy will become a lovable and reliable canine companion. Whenever visitors call, you should encourage them to gently pick up and handle your pup.

petting, care being taken that it is done in a manner which will not startle or frighten the puppy (in case the other participants are not experienced with handling canine youngsters). Visitors should be advised how important it is to start development of each puppy's personality along the right track, and that enjoyment of this attention helps the puppy to mature into a well-adjusted, happy, friendly animal. No Chow puppy should ever be left "just to grow"— he may then become cautious with strangers, of a hand stretched out to pet him, and of being picked up. Wariness of all people may develop.

As the puppies start to walk and move around a bit, they should be taught to play with people as well as with one another. The more human

puppies. Responsibly raised baby Chows are gently picked up, fondled, and talked to in soft, reassuring tones at least once or twice daily, which helps them to enjoy the presence of a human. As the puppy's eyes open, he learns to recognize people and looks forward to these times.

As soon as the puppies are a few weeks old, visitors come to see them (family members or friends), thus their socialization expands to include more than just owner and the puppies. At these times, each puppy should be picked up gently and handed to the guest for some

Once your Chow pup has had the first set of inoculations, he is ready to be acquainted with the great outdoors. Until he is fully vaccinated, it is a good idea to keep him around your home territory.

companionship a growing puppy enjoys, the better-adjusted he will be as a grown dog. A watchful eye must be kept upon the puppies as they play together, making certain that there is not a "bully" in the litter. Should there prove to be, and should that puppy really be rough on the others, it may be better to separate him/her from the rest of the litter (if slightly older puppies are available, they could join them at game time).

Once the puppies have had their first set of shots, and have begun to walk, they will begin leash training. Prior to receiving these shots, they should not be going to strange places where contagious diseases may be picked up. So until the first shots are attended to, they should be kept in and around their home territory.

A Chow puppy is now ready to be acquainted with the outside world. As an owner, you will enjoy teaching him that it is a good place, not at all scary, and that people are anxious to be friendly with him. After all, who but the most confirmed animal hater could possibly not fall "head over

Six-and-a-half-week-old Chow puppies playing together. A watchful eye should be kept on puppies as they play to make sure they don't cause too much mischief.

heels" for something as utterly adorable as a Chow puppy?

Let children and grown-ups pet the puppy gently, showing them how to extend the back of their hand for the puppy to sniff as an introduction. Allow those you feel sufficiently responsible to pick up and hold the puppy, but remember that, although puppies should be accustomed to being picked up, you do not want him to become frightened and be dropped or to struggle free from the holder's arms. Nor do you want him to panic and bite someone, so be careful to whom you extend picking-up privileges, and only do so when the puppy has made friends with that person on ground level first.

Teach the puppy to enjoy riding in the car. If you plan to travel with him to any extent, he should be taught to ride in a crate. Select a crate that will comfortably accommodate him as a fully grown dog as well as while a pup. Dogs are safest crated when carried in cars. Wire crates or those with interchangeable wood and wire panels are the best, as they can be made snug with the panels in cold weather and have better ventilation offered by the wire when needed during hot weather.

Take the puppy, as he grows, with you wherever he will be welcome. There is no better way of his learning to accept the outside world than by acquainting him with it.

Chow Chows fare especially well in city or suburban living, as they are not dogs who require excessive amounts of exercise or fields to roam. In the city, they manage quite well in the free run of your apartment with three or four daily "trips to the curb," augmented by a walk of several blocks with you, on lead, each day. They are fun to take around, as they do create both admiration and respect; the latter making your own safety on city streets far more likely.

Chows and children make the best of friends, seeming to have a natural affinity for one another. The ideal arrangement is to have the child and puppy grow up together, each growing to love and understand the other. As with a

Although Chow Chows do not require excessive exercise, they always appreciate a romp outdoors—especially with a friend.

dog of any breed, the child should be taught to be considerate of his pet; not to hurt the dog or be overly rough with him. It is wise to keep an eye on young friends as well as your own child, whenever they play with the pup or grown dog. Some children are unreasonably rough and hard on dogs and, in many cases, cause themselves to be bitten, which we all want to avoid.

There are many ways in which you can enjoy the companionship of your Chow Chow, starting, of course, with just having him around to love and admire. To this, working with him in obedience can be added. You can make a show dog of him if you have purchased a dog for this purpose or have selected a puppy with show potential. If so, you can also start your children off in Junior Showmanship. These are just a few of the possibilities.

It may amaze people who think of a Chow as independent and dignified to find that these dogs are quite trainable for obedience

Whether puppy or adult, Chow Chows who spend time outside should have the protection of a fenced-in yard.

Despite the fact that many people think of the Chow Chow as independent and dignified, he is quite trainable for obedience work.

with one who feigns deafness as you make commands or leisurely strolls off in the opposite direction, so start with a training class early. If you and the dog are working easily and well together, start entering him in obedience classes at your local dog shows when he reaches the eligible age (six months). If this does not prove to be a success, let it go—but it may be that your dog will have the talent to go through to the highest attainable titles if given the opportunity. In any event, he needs the basic training to obey the commands that are important to good canine citizenship. Another thing about working in obedience is that there is no better way in which one can develop a warm and lasting rapport with one's dog than by this method. You will be amazed at the warmth of love and loyalty developed through such cooperative activity. It is something that should not be missed by any dog owner!

work, and are well able to gain both CD and CDX degrees. It is a pity that more owners do not pursue these titles; just think how seldom we see a Chow competing in the obedience classes!

Basic obedience training should be a must on the agenda of every dog owner. It has been proven hundreds of times that instant obeying of the command to "sit" or "stay" has saved a dog's life. "Come," too, is a necessity of pleasant daily living, as are "down," and "heel." Your dog should be taught to obey these commands, whether or not you have an obedience career in mind for him.

When the puppy is a few months old, you and he should enroll in an obedience class, where the two of you will be taught the basics. Every dog owner owes this to himself and his pet. Life is far more enjoyable with a dog who will obey than

Whether or not you have a career in obedience in mind for your Chow, he should be taught to obey basic obedience commands such as "heel" and "come."

If you have a show future in mind for your dog, planning must start as a young puppy. In the Chow's case, the dog must be taught and accustomed to having his mouth held open in a very special way for examination (far more complicated for the Chow than just slipping the lips apart to see the "bite," as suffices in the opened; first the lips slipped apart in the front so the judge can see the "bite," then the jaws opened wide and held that way for a moment to give the judge the opportunity to see that both tongue and the roof of the mouth are black. The natural inclination is for dogs to resent this; so start early and repeat the examination

Many Chow Chows are able to gain degrees in obedience, as has this brilliant CDX Chow retrieving over a 26-inch high jump.

majority of breeds). With a Chow, the judge must be able to see and check the color of the tongue and of the roof of the mouth (which must be blue-black). Most prefer that the exhibitor do this, but some judges insist upon making the examination by opening the mouth personally. Thus your Chow's socialization must include a familiarity with this examination if he is to be a show dog. Throughout his puppyhood, he should be taught by repeated examination to have his mouth with frequency. Ideally, the dog should be educated on this point to the extent that either you or the judge will be able, with no fear of being bitten, to check the bite and examine the tongue and roof of mouth. A disqualification is involved here; hence the importance of it being possible to make a thorough examination, should the puppy become a show dog.

It is also necessary, in a show dog, that he be accustomed and agreeable to having his testicles

Chows make friends with other household pets if introduced properly. Avoid any problems of jealousy between the animals by giving them equal amounts of attention and affection.

checked, as AKC rules state that two must be normally descended or the dog disqualified. This is an area in which many Chows resent handling, so get started teaching the puppy to accept it as soon as he is on his feet.

Although heavy coated, Chows are little trouble as housedogs. They shed periodically, at which time they must have careful help in getting the dead coat out of the way. But they are clean, fastidious, non-destructive dogs who are to be trusted with a free run of the premises, even when you are not at home.

Although definitely not attack dogs, Chows are competent watchdogs who will bark an alarm. Meeting a Chow face-to-face will probably terrify any intruder who is not aware of the personality change of the modern Chow. Chows look forbidding with their characteristic scowling expression and they are obviously strong and powerful with their massive, muscular build. They are also identified, in many minds, with bad temper. Thus a prowler or burglar would do well to think twice before tangling with a Chow.

Chows make friends with other household pets if introduced tactfully. It is better, of course, if both or one or the other is a puppy or kitten; but even if not, with tact and avoidance of creating jealousy between the two (for your attention and affection), problems can be avoided. Remember that the animal already established in your home feels it is "his," and this must be respected by the newcomer until things get on a smooth-working basis.

CHOW CHOW DESCRIPTION

The Chow Chow is one of the world's most handsome dogs. It has several important physical characteristics combining to make the breed one of the most individual among all dogs. Only in the Chow Chow does one find the combination of solid black (or blue) tongue and mouth membrane, high-placed hocks and the stilted rear action they create, dignified scowling expression, and the squareness of build, all of which add up to the basic physical characteristics of the breed.

The Chow Chow is one of the world's most handsome dogs. His physical characteristics combine to give him a most individualistic expression.

One's first impression of a Chow Chow is that of a dog who is powerful, upstanding, heavily boned, squarely built with strong muscular development. His correct body is compact, broad and deep, its height measuring anywhere between 17 and 20 inches tall from the ground to the highest point of shoulder (withers). This measurement squares with the length of body which, measured from forechest to point of buttocks, should be equal. There is a tendency in the breed (presently being overcome) toward a longer body, which is a fault. This is a fact to be kept in mind if you are selecting a Chow Chow for either show or breeding purposes.

The short-coupled body is strong and deep, the chest reaching to the point of elbow, which distance should be halfway between the withers and ground. The topline is strong, muscular, and level; the short, broad croup made level by powerful rump and thigh muscles. The loin is deep, short and muscular. The standard of the breed notes that the "body, back, coupling and croup must all be short to create the required square build."

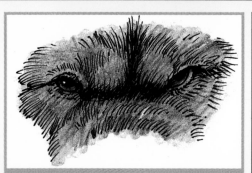

The Chow Chow's eyes should be deep set. The placement of the eyes is of utmost importance in creating the desirable Oriental expression. Drawing by John Quinn.

The proper tail is highset, follows the line of the spine at the start, and is carried closely to the back. It should be well feathered.

The head of the Chow Chow should be proudly carried on a strong, well-arched and muscular neck, the length of which is sufficient to carry the head nicely above the topline when the dog stands at attention. It should be large without exaggeration, fitting in nicely with the overall balance of the dog. The topskull is flat, with toplines of skull and muzzle approximately parallel when viewed in profile, joined by a moderate stop. The muzzle should be at least one-third of the total length of head; broad, and well filled out beneath the eyes. The width and depth of the muzzle should equal one another, carrying out to the tip; this squareness is achieved by correct bone structure combined with padding of the muzzle and well-cushioned lips. It should be remembered, however, that excess padding of the muzzle, to the extent of making it appear other than square in shape, is

undesirable. Upper lips should never be pendulous, but should completely cover the lower lips when the mouth is closed.

The nose of the Chow Chow has well-opened nostrils and is large, broad, and black, the only deviation from the black color being in blue Chows, where noses which are slate or blue are permissible.

A solid black mouth is ideal, with edges of the lips and tissues of the mouth mostly black; black gums are preferred. The top surface and edges of the tongue should be solid black (or blue), the darker the better. The teeth should be strong and level with a scissors bite (in which the inner tips of the upper incisors touch the outer tips of the lower incisors).

The eyes are dark brown, deep set, almond in shape, obliquely placed, and of moderate size. The correct shape, size, and placement of the eyes is of utmost importance in creating the desirable Oriental expression. Eyes and rims are black, with lids that neither droop nor turn in,

The ears of the Chow Chow should be triangular in shape, rounding slightly at the tip. Drawing by John Quinn.

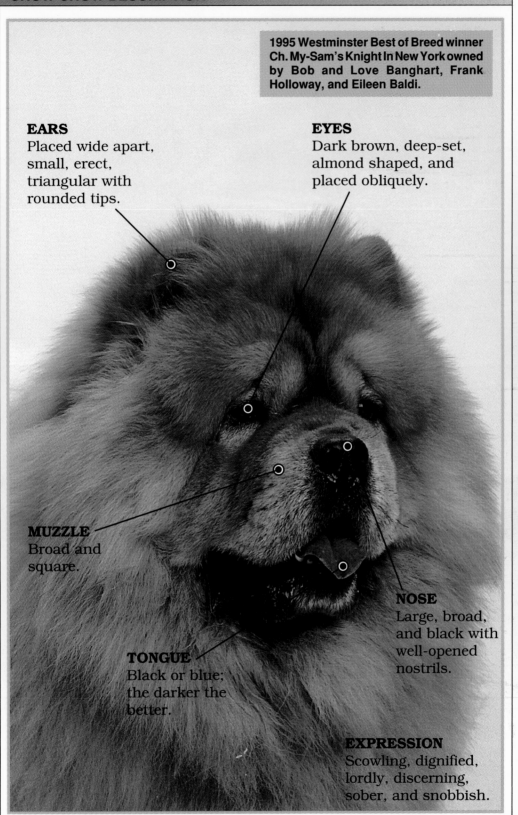

1995 Westminster Best of Breed winner Ch. My-Sam's Knight In New York owned by Bob and Love Banghart, Frank Holloway, and Eileen Baldi.

EARS
Placed wide apart, small, erect, triangular with rounded tips.

EYES
Dark brown, deep-set, almond shaped, and placed obliquely.

MUZZLE
Broad and square.

NOSE
Large, broad, and black with well-opened nostrils.

TONGUE
Black or blue; the darker the better.

EXPRESSION
Scowling, dignified, lordly, discerning, sober, and snobbish.

and the pupils of the eyes should be clearly visible.

A Chow Chow's ears are placed wide apart, with the inner corner being on top of the skull. They should be small in size, of moderate thickness, and carried stiffly erect with a slight forward tilt. They are triangular in shape, rounding slightly at the tip. A correct Chow Chow ear never flops as the dog moves; and a drop ear, or one that breaks at any point between base and tip or is carried other than stiffly erect, disqualifies the dog from competition in the show ring.

The Chow Chow's expression is scowling, dignified, lordly, discerning, sober, and snobbish, creating a look of independence. Its components are: a marked brow, with a padded button skin just above the inside upper corner of each eye; a sufficient play of skin to form a frown at the brows; a distinct furrow between the eyes that begins at the base of the muzzle and continues up the forehead; a correctly formed and placed eye;

The Chow expression creates a look of independence. It is marked by a sufficient play of skin to form a frown at the brows.

and correct shape, carriage and placement of the ear. Excessive loose skin is undesirable, and wrinkles on the muzzle, since they do not contribute to expression, are not desired.

The forequarters of the Chow Chow are well muscled, with tips of the shoulder blades placed moderately close together. The upper arm is never less than the length of shoulder blade, with elbows set well back alongside the chest wall, turning neither in nor out as the dog moves. Forelegs are perfectly straight and heavily boned from elbow to foot, parallel and widely spaced in keeping with the wide chest. Pasterns are short and upright, with no tendency toward knuckling. The Chow Chow stands well up on round, catlike feet which are thickly padded. Dewclaws may be removed.

The rear assembly of a Chow Chow is broad and powerful, with well-muscled hips and thighs and heavy bone which approximately equals that of the forequarters. From behind, the legs are straight and parallel to one another, rather widely spaced owing to the broad pelvis. There is little angulation at the stifle joint, which is strong, well knit and firm. The hock joint, although well let down, appears almost straight. These are the components of the correct, individualistic stilted action, therefore of particular importance. The hock joint must be firm, strong and well knit, free of any inclination to bend or break in any direction. The metatarsals are short and perpendicular to the

The Chow Chow is a powerful, upstanding, heavily boned dog that is squarely built with strong muscular development.

ground. The feet, as in the front, are round and catlike.

The typical Chow Chow gait is straight moving and agile, sound, quick, and powerful. The dog should not appear to lumber along; nor should he "side-wind." The rear gait is short and stilted due to the straight assemblage of the legs, moving up and forward from the hip in a somewhat pendulum-like manner, with a slight bounce in the rump. The strong thrust to the hind foot transfers power to the body in an almost straight line, its efficient transmission to the forequarters requiring the short coupling important to the breed, which permits no "roll" to the mid-section of the dog. In moving, as speed increases the forelegs incline slightly inward from their otherwise exactly parallel placement. At the same time the hindlegs come slightly closer together.

The Chow Chow Club of America received approval for a change in its Breed Standard of Points effective November 11, 1986, thus adding the smooth coated Chow Chow to the long-recognized rough coat which, for years, has been considered here to be indigenous to the breed.

Actually, smooth coated Chows have long been known and loved in many parts of the world, and have had a strong group of fanciers working for their continuation in Europe, the United States, and elsewhere. We are told that smooth Chow Chows are as normal as the roughs and since it is a member of the Chow family, it should not be neglected. Smooth Chow Chows must compete in the show ring under the same standard, except as regards coat, with the rough

the coat is hard and dense, consisting of a smooth outer coat over a definite under coat, with no obvious ruff or feathering on the legs or tail.

The rough coated Chow Chow, on the other hand, is covered with an abundance of dense, outstanding, straight, somewhat

Among the five Chow colors are cream and red. Reds can be anywhere from a pale golden to a deep mahogany.

Chow Chows. This is not easy for them, as they lack that glamorous finishing touch of the abundant, offstanding coat and mane that has become synonymous with Chow Chow beauty. Nonetheless, there are already American Champions in the breed (as there are title holders in some of the other countries where they are recognized) and the dogs are of very nice quality.

In the smooth coated variety,

coarse outer coat over a soft, thick, and wooly undercoat. A profuse ruff is formed around the head and neck, usually thicker and longer in dogs than in bitches. Since coat length is variable in the individual Chow, emphasis should be placed on texture, thickness, and condition of the coat rather than on its length.

Trimming of the whiskers, feet and metatarsus is optional and permissible, but a word of

Although the smooth coat variety was only added to the Chow Chow standard in 1986, this variety has been long known in many parts of the world. Smooths compete in the show ring under the same standard except with regards to coat.

The smooth Chow has a hard, dense coat, with no obvious ruff or feathering on the legs or tail.

warning to those showing this breed: over-trimming is not desired, as in many cases it makes the dog look mutilated rather than more beautiful, and should not be encouraged.

Chows are a clear-colored breed, five colors being acceptable without preference. These are red (pale golden to deep mahogany), black, blue, cinnamon (light fawn to deep cinnamon), and cream.

Disqualifications for Chow Chows to be shown in AKC competition are as follows: nose spotted or distinctly other color than black, except in blue Chows, which may have solid blue or slate noses; the top surface or edges of the tongue red or pink, or with one or more spots of red or pink; drop ear or ears. A drop ear is one which breaks at any point from its base to its tip, or which is not carried stiffly erect but lies parallel to the top of the skull.

In speaking of these disqualifications, the writer wishes to place emphasis on the fact that they are of concern to people who are interested in *breeding* or in *exhibiting* Chows *only*. A breeder, obviously, does not wish to perpetuate a disqualifying fault, and an exhibitor will face the embarrassment of disqualification in the show ring with such a dog.

However, there is nothing about any of these disqualifications that affects the good health or well-being of the dog. So, if you are choosing it purely as a pet or family companion, do not hesitate to select a Chow that may have a disqualifying condition if the dog appeals to you and the price is right. Such faults may occasionally appear in even the finest breeding programs; and dogs possessing them should be available to good homes at a lesser price than a dog of show or breeding quality. So do not close your mind to this possibility. A reliable breeder will point out a disqualifying feature to a prospective purchaser and the price will be adjusted accordingly. Thus you are getting a well-bred, well raised, and healthy dog (from a conscientious breeder) who will make just as splendid a companion as a dog who is perfect in show ring

World-renowned Chow Chow judge Dr. Samuel Draper and handler Desmond Murphy are the geniuses behind Liontamer Chows. This is Lov-Chow's Risen Star. At Liontamer, the standard is reached for in every litter—in temperament as well as sound conformation.

qualifications. Why not take advantage of this fact if you really take to the dog and are not planning a show or breeding career for it? Breeders will usually request that such bitches be spayed, which is best for their health anyway and is recommended for all such Chows *not* being bred or shown.

THE BREED STANDARD

A breed standard is the criterion by which the appearance (and to a certain extent, the temperament as well) of any given dog is made subject to objective measurement. Basically, the standard for any breed is a definition of the perfect dog, to which all specimens of the breed are compared. Breed standards are always subject to change through review by the national breed club for each dog, so it is always wise to keep up with developments in a breed by checking the publications of your national kennel club.

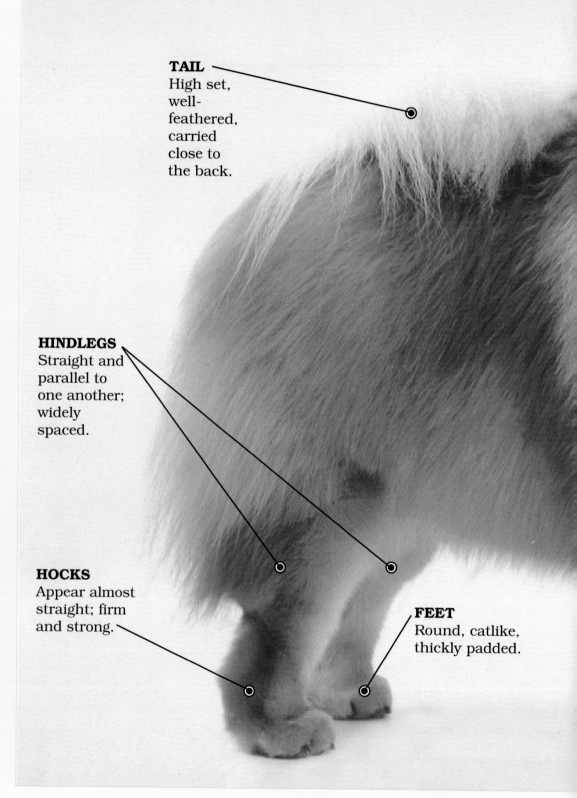

1995 Westminster Best of Breed winner Ch. My-Sam's Knight In New York owned by Bob and Love Banghart, Frank Holloway, and Eileen Baldi.

TAIL
High set, well-feathered, carried close to the back.

HINDLEGS
Straight and parallel to one another; widely spaced.

HOCKS
Appear almost straight; firm and strong.

FEET
Round, catlike, thickly padded.

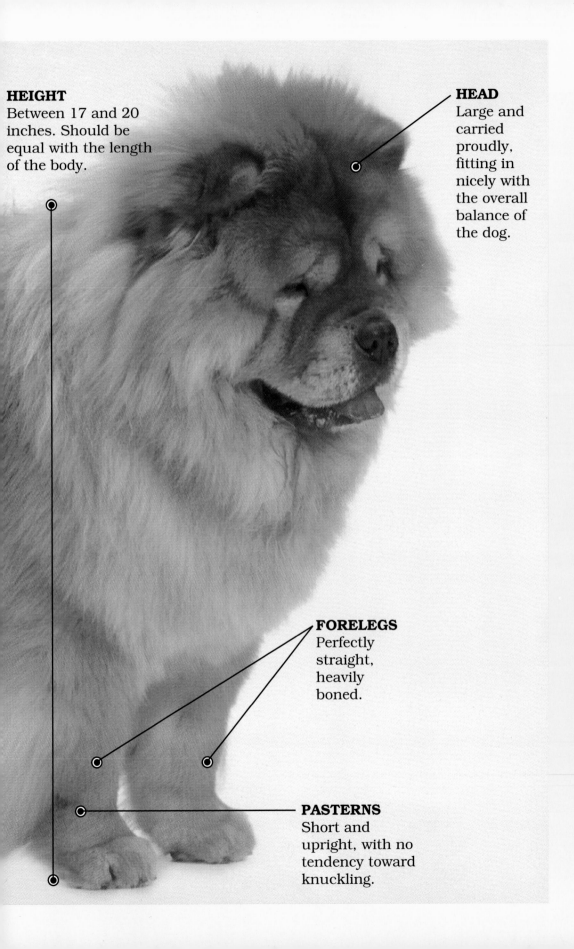

HEIGHT
Between 17 and 20 inches. Should be equal with the length of the body.

HEAD
Large and carried proudly, fitting in nicely with the overall balance of the dog.

FORELEGS
Perfectly straight, heavily boned.

PASTERNS
Short and upright, with no tendency toward knuckling.

YOUR CHOW CHOW PUPPY

SELECTION

When you do pick out a Chow Chow puppy as a pet, don't be hasty; the longer you study puppies, the better you will understand them. Make it your transcendent concern to select only one that radiates good health your protective instinct. *Pick the Chow Chow puppy who forthrightly picks you! The feeling of attraction should be mutual!*

DOCUMENTS

Now, a little paper work is in order. When you purchase a

The longer you study Chow puppies, the better you'll understand them, and the easier your final decision will be!

and spirit and is lively on his feet, whose eyes are bright, whose coat shines, and who comes forward eagerly to make and to cultivate your acquaintance. Don't fall for any shy little darling that wants to retreat to his bed or his box, or plays coy behind other puppies or people, or hides his head under your arm or jacket appealing to

purebred Chow Chow puppy, you should receive a transfer of ownership, registration material, and other "papers" (a list of the immunization shots, if any, the puppy may have been given; a note on whether or not the puppy has been wormed; a diet and feeding schedule to which the puppy is accustomed) and you are welcomed as a fellow owner to a long, pleasant association with a most lovable pet, and more (news)paper work.

GENERAL PREPARATION

You have chosen to own a particular Chow Chow puppy. You have chosen it very carefully over all other breeds and all other puppies. So before you ever get that Chow Chow puppy home, you will have prepared for its arrival by reading everything you can get your hands on having to do with the management of Chow Chows and puppies. True, you will run into many conflicting opinions, but at least you will not be starting "blind." Read, study, digest. Talk over your plans with your veterinarian, other "Chow Chow people," and the seller of your Chow Chow puppy.

When you get your Chow Chow puppy, you will find that your reading and studying are far from finished. You've just scratched the surface in your plan

Pick a Chow puppy that exhibits good health and spirit, with bright eyes and a shiny coat.

to provide the greatest possible comfort and health for your Chow Chow; and, by the same token, you do want to assure yourself of the greatest possible enjoyment of this wonderful creature. You must be ready for this puppy mentally as well as in the physical requirements.

TRANSPORTATION

If you take the puppy home by car, protect him from drafts, particularly in cold weather. Wrapped in a towel and carried in the arms or lap of a passenger, the Chow Chow puppy will usually make the trip without mishap. If the pup starts to drool and to squirm, stop the car for a few minutes. Have newspapers handy in case of car-sickness. A covered carton lined with newspapers provides protection for puppy and car, if you are driving alone. Avoid excitement and unnecessary handling of the puppy on arrival. A Chow Chow puppy is a very small "package" to be making a complete change of surroundings and company, and he needs frequent rest and refreshment to renew his vitality.

THE FIRST DAY AND NIGHT

When your Chow Chow puppy arrives in your home, put him down on the floor and don't pick him up again, except when it is absolutely necessary. He is a dog, a real dog, and must not be lugged around like a rag doll. Handle him as little as possible, and permit no one to pick him up and baby him. To repeat, *put your Chow Chow puppy on the floor or the ground and let him stay there*

Your Chow puppy should have a bed of his own placed in a warm area that is free from drafts.

Color is another consideration—how about an adorable black Chow puppy?

except when it may be necessary to do otherwise.

Quite possibly your Chow Chow puppy will be afraid for a while in his new surroundings, without his mother and littermates. Comfort him and reassure him, but don't console him. Don't give him the "oh-you-poor-itsy-bitsy-puppy" treatment. Be calm, friendly, and reassuring. Encourage him to walk around and sniff over his new home. If it's dark, put on the lights. Let him roam for a few minutes while you and everyone else concerned sit quietly or go about your routine business. Let the puppy come back to you.

Playmates may cause an immediate problem if the new Chow Chow puppy is to be greeted by children or other pets. If not, you can skip this subject. The natural affinity between puppies and children calls for some supervision until a live-and-let-live relationship is established.

This applies particularly to a Christmas puppy, when there is more excitement than usual and more chance for a puppy to swallow something upsetting. It is a better plan to welcome the puppy several days before or after the holiday week. Like a baby, your Chow Chow puppy needs much rest and should not be over-handled. Once a child realizes that a puppy has "feelings" similar to his own, and since its floor can usually be easily cleaned. Let him explore the kitchen to his heart's content; close doors to confine him there. Prepare his food and feed him lightly the first night. Give him a pan with some water in it—not a lot, since most puppies will try to drink the whole pan dry. Give him an old coat or shirt to lie on. Since a coat or shirt will be strong in human scent, he will pick it out to lie on, thus furthering his feeling

A trio of smooth Chow puppies. If grooming is a concern, consider a smooth Chow—the grooming responsibilities are much less involved than those of rough Chows.

can readily be hurt or injured, the opportunities for play and responsibilities provide exercise and training for both.

For his first night with you, he should be put where he is to sleep every night—say in the kitchen, of security in the room where he has just been fed.

HOUSEBREAKING HELPS

Now, sooner or later—mostly sooner—your new Chow Chow puppy is going to "puddle" on the

Who could possibly not fall "head over heels" for something as adorable as a Chow puppy?

floor. First take a newspaper and lay it on the puddle until the urine is soaked up onto the paper. *Save this paper.* Now take a cloth with soap and water, wipe up the floor and dry it well. Then take the wet paper and place it on a fairly large square of newspapers in a convenient corner. When cleaning up, always keep a piece of wet paper on top of the others. Every time he wants to "squat," he will seek out this spot and use the papers. (This routine is rarely necessary for more than three days.) Now leave your Chow Chow puppy for the night. Quite probably he will cry and howl a bit; some are more stubborn than others on this matter. But let him stay alone for the night. This may seem harsh treatment, but it is the best procedure in the long run. Just let him cry; he will weary of it sooner or later.

GROOMING YOUR CHOW CHOW

A Chow Chow is a dog who requires considerable coat care, whether for the show ring or as a pet, so if you are a "brush lazy" person, be very certain that this is a matter with which you can cope before purchasing. It is true that Chows need frequent bathing, as dirt accumulating in the coat can cause scratching, leading to skin irritations or sore spots. In addition, the thick, soft undercoat is of a texture which mats easily; the best manner of handling mats is prevention of their forming or catching them at a very early stage, rather than trying to work them out or being forced to cut them away (which will leave "holes" in the dog's coat) once they have become a reality.

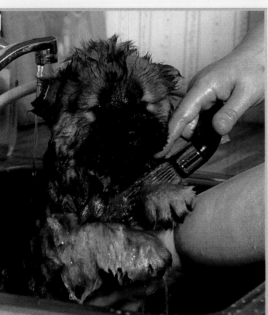

Chow Chows need frequent bathing so acclimate your puppy to this procedure at a young age. Use comfortably warm water and a spray hose.

To bathe your Chow Chow, stand him firmly on a rubber mat in a tub (so that his feet will "ground" and he will not slip) after having thoroughly brushed out his coat to remove loose hair.

Place a drop of castor or mineral oil in each eye to prevent soap irritation, and a wad of dry cotton in each ear to prevent water entering the ear canal.

Now you are ready to thoroughly wet the dog down, using comfortably (test it on your wrist) warm water and a rubber shampoo spray hose. Work from behind the ears on backward to the tail. Once the coat is soaked with warm water, apply a good quality shampoo made especially for this purpose, or a baby shampoo if you prefer. This shampoo should be worked into the coat and skin with your hands, lathering up briskly but gently. Rinse well, then apply a second sudsing, repeating the process of lathering and rinsing. Remember that the second rinsing must be extremely thorough, as traces of even the mildest soap remaining on the skin can cause scratching and irritation. If you

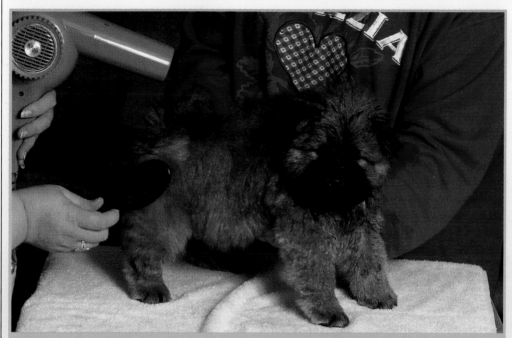

When you dry your Chow, use an electric hair-dryer set on *warm* not hot. It is also important to brush the dog while drying.

have a problem with fleas, lice, or ticks, by all means select a high quality pesticide shampoo with which to bathe the dog, using one recommended by your veterinarian or the breeder of your dog. In shopping for any products to be used on your Chow, *read labels carefully and heed any warnings having to do with reaction possibilities.*

Many owners like using either a shampoo-conditioner or a cream rinse on their rough coated Chows, which should be selected carefully and directions followed exactly. With the rinses as well as with the shampoo, be certain that you have removed all traces of the preparation from the coat before considering that the dog is *thoroughly* and *correctly* rinsed.

To rinse the dog's head, the easiest and best method is to hold the muzzle firmly, tilting it upward, then allow the warm water from your hose to run down the head and back of neck from above the eyes. The foreface and chin can be rinsed from underneath. The head, of course, must be rinsed as thoroughly as the body of the dog.

When your Chow is washed and rinsed to your satisfaction, blot out the excess water with a couple of large Turkish towels. *Blot,* don't *rub,* especially on a rough Chow, as a rubbing motion with the towel will start tangles. Blotting, and a good shake or two, should do a good job of removing excess water, readying the dog for the electric hair-dryer, which should be handy and which is a most important piece of equipment for proper Chow Chow coat care. Be certain to set the dryer on "warm" rather than "hot" as a precaution against an uncomfortable degree of heat on the dog.

You may, in warm weather, permit a pet Chow to dry naturally outside in the sun, but it is a *must* for a show dog (and better for any dog), particularly in the case of the rough coated Chow, that you *brush* the dog dry under the hair blower.

The grooming of your Chow Chow should start at an early age, as then the entire process will seem perfectly natural and not be so easily resented by the grown dog. Whether your Chow is rough or smooth coated, a show dog or a pet, frequent (gentle, of course) grooming from as young an age as four weeks can and should be part of your schedule.

The most important part of caring for a Chow Chow coat (the rough variety especially) is frequent and *correct* brushing. One must part the hair in methodical rows as one works, about half-an-inch apart at a time, brushing (always with the skin clearly visible) from the roots of the hairs to the tips.

A grooming table is one of the most useful of all pieces of equipment for an owner of a "coated" breed. These tables, which fold neatly for easy storage or transportation, are topped with rubber, which prevents slipping as you work on the dog, and are provided with an "arm" from which a "noose" dangles, the latter being placed around the dog's neck to ground him firmly

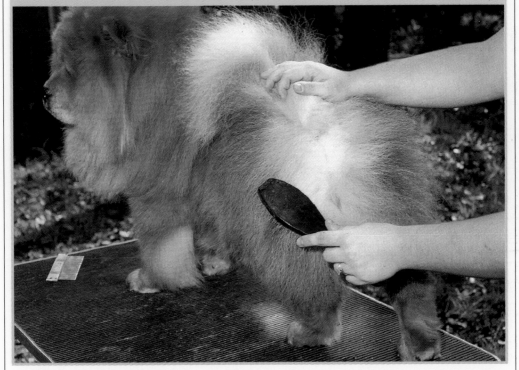

You should always brush your Chow Chow with the skin clearly visible from the roots of the hairs to the tips.

while you are working on him. This is especially handy for such details as nail clipping, tooth scraping, whisker trimming, eye cleaning, and ear care—in fact for *any* situation where sudden lurching could cause a problem.

For brushing your rough coated Chow, you will need a "pin brush" plus a wire slicker or "rake." Other necessities include a high grade coat conditioner, either an aerosol or spray; a pair of scissors, which are preferably curved at the tips to avoid accidents; and a steel comb, for helping to separate any new mats you may find and for putting final touches on the thoroughly brushed coat.

A steel comb is helpful for separating mats as well as putting the finishing touches on a thoroughly brushed coat.

As young as one month, a puppy can be taught to lie on his side on the grooming table to be brushed. Make it a pleasant time for the puppy by talking to him and petting as you work, but make it clear that this is *business* and that brushing is an important thing in the life of a Chow. Starting young will give you a decided advantage in having a dog who takes grooming as a matter of course. As the puppy, or grown dog, lies on his side, the entire underneath and each side of the dog can be easily reached and worked on. When one side is finished, turn the dog to the other side for the second part of the grooming.

Start at the withers with a pin brush, making a part *clear through to the skin* across the side of the dog. With the pin brush, brush the coat thoroughly, *from the skin out,* from both sides of the part (this should take about ten minutes for each part). Then move on to the *next* area, about half-an-inch ahead of the one on which you've been working, and repeat the process. Keep your parts *close* so that no area gets skipped, and keep repeating the process until you have worked your way to the rear end of the dog. Then, for step two, move to the other side of the table and repeat the process in reverse, just as thoroughly, working your way back to the dog's front end. Upon finishing this side completely, turn the dog over (let him off the table for a few moments to relax) to his other side, and repeat the entire process. As you work, keep an eye out for possible starts of tangles that might grow into mats in the armpits, between the hindquarters, or behind the ears. Any mats should be untangled

allow the dog to sit or stand on the grooming table while his mane, legs, and tail are done. Then, as a finishing touch, brush the dog's coat in reverse (from tail to head), as a last minute "refresher," to show every hair to best advantage.

Remember that only a *minimal* amount of trimming should be

This drawing shows the proper method of grooming the Chow Chow. The arrows show the direction in which the hair should be brushed. Drawing by John Quinn.

with your comb and fingers if at all possible; only as a last resort should a mat be cut away.

When you are satisfied that the sides and underneath portions of the dog have been carefully done,

done on a Chow Chow, even for the show ring. The whiskers may be trimmed if one wishes. The feet may be trimmed around the edges to "neaten" their round, cat-like appearance. And hair from

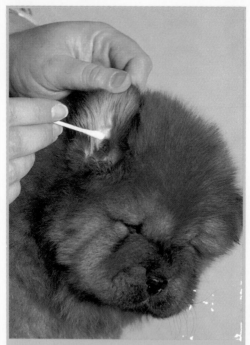

You can clean your Chow's ears with a cotton swab soaked in hydrogen peroxide or an ear-cleansing lotion available at your local pet shop. Be careful not to stick the cotton swab too far into the ear.

dog is scratching an ear, or shaking his head frequently or holding it to one side, there may be ear mites or some other infection. Rinse the ear out with peroxide, then apply a medicated ointment (available through your veterinarian or by prescription only) if the ear looks red, is oozing, or has any odor. This should clear the condition up promptly; if not, have your veterinarian see the dog.

Teeth should be inspected regularly for signs of tartar. Learning to use a handy little gadget called a "tooth scraper" can prove very useful; this must be done with gentleness and care so as not to injure the gums whenever you see tartar

You can clean around your Chow's eyes by gently wiping them with a damp cloth.

between the pads underneath the foot should be cleared away for the dog's comfort and to avoid foot ailments. Excessive clearing away of hair at the base of the tail creates an unattractive appearance and is very obvious in most cases. It does *not* make the dog appear shorter backed—only distorted—to the person judging the dog. However, it may be necessary, to some extent, for sanitary reasons; if that is the case, it should be done with *restraint* lest the coat look "butchered."

Other grooming areas include ear care and the teeth. Chows are not prone to ear problems, but an occasional dusting of medicated ear powder does no harm. If the accumulating. Learn the proper use of this tooth scraper from your veterinarian or the breeder of your dog.

This coat care program is intended for owners of rough coated Chows, the type that is better known and more popular at this time. This program presents the basics, from keeping your Chow's coat clean, healthy, and presentable to preparing a dog of gleaming beauty for the show ring. How many of the suggestions you follow depend on what your plans are for the dog, and while it is not necessary to go to such lengths in caring for your pet, there is a sense of pride and satisfaction in making your dog look his very best. Let me caution,

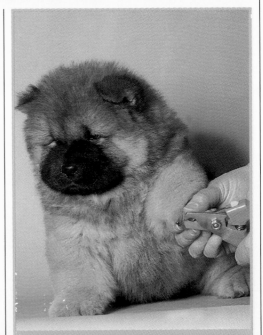

Clipping your puppy's nails should begin at a young age so he becomes used to the procedure. If you are unsure of yourself at first, let your veterinarian show you how.

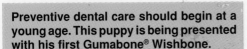

Preventive dental care should begin at a young age. This puppy is being presented with his first Gumabone® Wishbone.

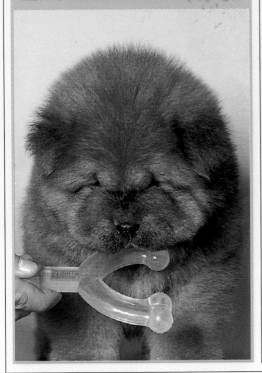

please, against neglect of the rough Chow Chow coat: Once it becomes seriously matted, there is often no correction possible except to shave down the dog, which is a pity. So, even if you do not have the time or patience to go through the suggested routine with your pet, do make it an absolute must that he be bathed when he looks or smells dirty, and that you do get to brush him at least every few days. Just be sure that you do brush methodically and *to the skin*, with no areas being skipped in which "hot spots" can form.

Grooming a smooth coated Chow is a far less complex job. Even bathing should be less frequent, as it will soften the desired hard, smooth outer coat.

FEEDING

Now let's talk about feeding your Chow Chow, a subject so simple that it's amazing there is so much nonsense and misunderstanding about it. Is it expensive to feed a Chow Chow? No, it is not! You can feed your high degree of selectivity in their food, and unless you spoil them with great variety (and possibly turn them into poor, "picky" eaters) they will eat almost anything that they become accustomed to. Many dogs flatly

When you first bring your Chow puppy home, it is a good idea to continue to feed him what he is used to eating. If you wish to change the food, do so gradually.

Chow Chow economically and keep him in perfect shape the year round, or you can feed him expensively. He'll thrive either way, and let's see why this is true.

First of all, remember a Chow Chow is a dog. Dogs do not have a refuse to eat nice, fresh beef. They pick around it and eat everything else. But meat—bah! Why? They aren't accustomed to it! They'd eat rabbit fast enough, but they refuse beef because they aren't used to it.

VARIETY NOT NECESSARY

A good general rule of thumb is forget all human preferences and don't give a thought to variety. Choose the right diet for your Chow Chow and feed it to him day after day, year after year, winter and summer. But what is the right diet?

Hundreds of thousands of dollars have been spent in canine the basic diet most often recommended is one that consists of a dry food, either meal or kibble form. There are several of excellent quality, manufactured by reliable companies, research tested, and nationally advertised. They are inexpensive, highly satisfactory, and easily available in stores everywhere in containers of five to 50 pounds. Larger

It is okay for two Chow puppies to share a dish when they are still young; however, as they get bigger they will definitely need separate food and water dishes.

nutrition research. The results are pretty conclusive, so you needn't go into a lot of experimenting with trials of this and that every other week. Research has proven just what your dog needs to eat to keep healthy.

DOG FOOD

There are almost as many right diets as there are dog experts, but amounts cost less per pound, usually.

If you have a choice of brands, it is usually safer to choose the better known one; but even so, carefully read the analysis on the package. Do not choose any food in which the protein level is less than 25 percent, and be sure that this protein comes from both animal and vegetable sources. The good dog foods have meat meal, fish meal, liver, and such, plus protein from alfalfa and soy beans, as well as some dried-milk product. Note the vitamin content carefully. See that they are all there in good proportions; and be especially certain that the food contains properly high levels of vitamins A and D, two of the most perishable and important ones. Note the B-complex level, but don't worry about carbohydrate and mineral levels. These substances are plentiful and cheap and not likely to be lacking in a good brand.

For no-mess feeding, a feeding tray is very practical. Feeding trays are available in different styles and colors at your local pet shop. Photo courtesy of Penn Plax.

Some breeders recommend that you supplement your dog's food with natural meats, vegetables, etc; while others prefer to use vitamin supplements available at pet shops; some use both; others use none.

The advice given for how to choose a dry food also applies to moist or canned types of dog foods, if you decide to feed one of these.

Having chosen a really good food, feed it to your Chow Chow as the manufacturer directs. And once you've started, stick to it. Never change if you can possibly help it. A switch from one meal or kibble-type food can usually be made without too much upset; however, a change will almost invariably give you (and your Chow Chow) some trouble.

WHEN SUPPLEMENTS ARE NEEDED

Now what about supplements of various kinds, mineral and vitamin, or the various oils? They are all okay to add to your Chow Chow's food. However, if you are feeding your Chow Chow a correct diet, and this is easy to do, no supplements are necessary unless your Chow Chow has been improperly fed, has been sick, or is having puppies. Vitamins and minerals are naturally present in all the foods; and to ensure against any loss through processing, they are added in concentrated form to the dog food you use. Except on the advice of your veterinarian, added amounts of vitamins can prove harmful to your Chow Chow! The same risk goes with minerals.

directions on the food package. Your own Chow Chow may want a little more or a little less.

Fresh, cool water should always be available to your Chow Chow. This is important to good health throughout his lifetime.

Stainless steel food and water dishes are probably the best for your Chow Chow. They are sturdy and easy to clean.

FEEDING SCHEDULE

When and how much food to give your Chow Chow? As to when (except in the instance of puppies), suit yourself. You may feed two meals per day or the same amount in one single feeding, either morning or night. As to how to prepare the food and how much to give, it is generally best to follow the

ALL CHOW CHOWS NEED TO CHEW

Puppies and young Chow Chows need something with resistance to chew on while their teeth and jaws are developing—for cutting the puppy teeth, to induce growth of the permanent teeth under the puppy teeth, to assist in getting rid of the puppy teeth at the proper time, to help the permanent teeth through the

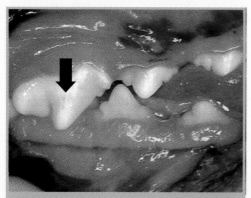

A scientific study shows a dog's tooth (arrow) while being maintained by Gumabone® chewing.

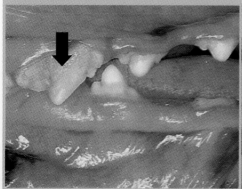

The Gumabone® was taken away and in 30 days the tooth (arrow) was almost completely covered with plaque and tartar.

provide your Chow Chow with something to chew—something that has the necessary functional qualities, is desirable from the Chow Chow's viewpoint, and is safe for him.

It is very important that your Chow Chow not be permitted to chew on anything he can break or on any indigestible thing from which he can bite sizable chunks. Sharp pieces, such as from a bone which can be broken by a dog, may pierce the intestinal wall and kill. Indigestible things that can be bitten off in chunks, such as from shoes or rubber or plastic toys, may cause an intestinal stoppage (if not regurgitated) and bring painful death, unless surgery is promptly performed.

Strong natural bones, such as 4- to 8-inch lengths of round shin bone from mature beef—either the kind you can get from a butcher or one of the variety available commercially in pet stores—may serve your Chow

gums, to ensure normal jaw development, and to settle the permanent teeth solidly in the jaws.

The adult Chow Chow's desire to chew stems from the instinct for tooth cleaning, gum massage, and jaw exercise—plus the need for an outlet for periodic doggie tensions.

This is why dogs, especially puppies and young dogs, will often destroy property worth hundreds of dollars when their chewing instinct is not diverted from their owner's possessions. And this is why you should

Pet shops sell real bones that have been colored, cooked, dyed or served natural. Although these are large, they are easily destroyed and can become very dangerous.

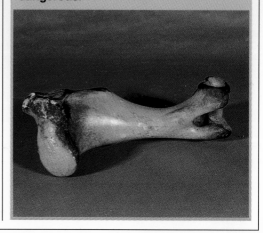

Chow's teething needs if his mouth is large enough to handle them effectively. You may be tempted to give your Chow Chow puppy a smaller bone and he may not be able to break it when you do, but puppies grow rapidly and the power of their jaws constantly increases until maturity. This means that a growing Chow Chow may break one of the smaller bones at any time, swallow the pieces, and die painfully before you realize what is wrong.

All hard natural bones are very abrasive. If your Chow Chow is an avid chewer, natural bones may wear away his teeth prematurely; hence, they then should be taken away from your dog when the teething purposes have been served. The badly worn, and usually painful, teeth of many mature dogs can be traced to excessive chewing on natural bones.

The Nylabone® provides your Chow Chow with hours of entertainment while brightening his teeth and spirits.

Contrary to popular belief, knuckle bones that can be chewed up and swallowed by your Chow Chow provide little, if any, usable calcium or other nutriment. They do, however, disturb the digestion of most dogs and cause them to vomit the nourishing food they need.

Dried rawhide products of various types, shapes, sizes, and prices are available on the market and have become quite popular. However, they don't serve the primary chewing functions very well; they are a bit messy when wet from mouthing, and most Chow Chows chew them up rather rapidly—but they have been considered safe for dogs until recently. Now, more and more incidents of death, and near death, by strangulation have been reported to be the results of partially swallowed chunks of rawhide swelling in the throat.

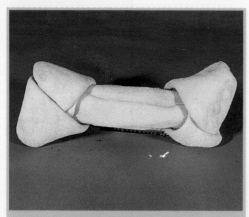

Rawhide is probably the best-selling dog chew. It can be dangerous and cause a dog to choke on it as it swells when wet.

confuse this with pressed rawhide, which is nothing more than small strips of rawhide squeezed together.

The nylon bones, especially those with natural meat and bone fractions added, are probably the most complete, safe, and economical answer to the chewing need. Dogs cannot break them or bite off sizable chunks; hence, they are completely safe—and being longer lasting than other things offered for the purpose, they are economical.

Hard chewing raises little bristle-like projections on the surface of the nylon bones—to provide effective interim tooth cleaning and vigorous gum massage, much in the same way your toothbrush does it for you. The little projections are raked off and swallowed in the form of thin shavings, but the chemistry of the nylon is such that they break down in the stomach fluids and pass through without effect.

More recently, some veterinarians have been attributing cases of acute constipation to large pieces of incompletely digested rawhide in the intestine.

A new product, molded rawhide, is very safe. During the process, the rawhide is melted and then injection molded into the familiar dog shape. It is very hard and is eagerly accepted by Chow Chows. The melting process also sterilizes the rawhide. Don't

Molded rawhide, called Roarhide® by Nylabone®, is very hard and safe for your dog. It is eagerly accepted by Chow Chows.

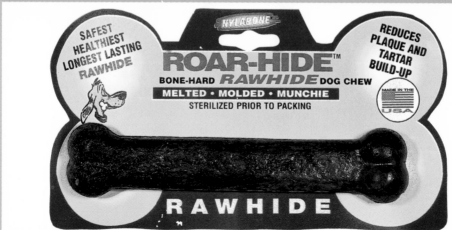

A Gumabone® after chewing. The knobs develop elastic frays that act as a toothbrush.

A Gumabone® before chewing. The dog slowly chews off the knobs.

The Galileo™ by Nylabone® is an extremely tough nylon pacifier. Its design is based upon original sketches by Galileo himself.

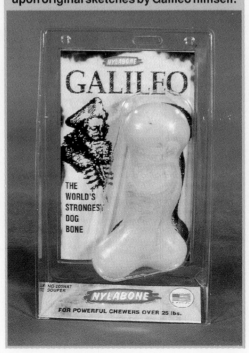

The nylon tug-toy is actually a dental floss. You grab one end and let your Chow pull at the other as it slowly slips through his teeth since nylon is self-lubricating.

The toughness of the nylon provides the strong chewing resistance needed for important jaw exercise and effectively aids teething functions, but there is no tooth wear because nylon is non-abrasive. Being inert, nylon does not support the growth of microorganisms; and it can be washed in soap and water or it can be sterilized by boiling or in an autoclave.

Nylabone® is highly recommended by veterinarians as a safe, healthy nylon bone that can't splinter or chip. Nylabone® is frizzled by the dog's chewing action, creating a toothbrush-like surface that cleanses the teeth and massages the gums. Nylabone®, the only chew products made of flavor-impregnated solid nylon, are available in your local pet shop. Nylabone® is superior to the cheaper bones because it is made of virgin nylon, which is the strongest and longest-lasting type of nylon available. The cheaper bones are made from recycled or re-ground nylon scraps, and have a tendency to break apart and split easily.

Nothing, however, substitutes for periodic professional attention for your Chow Chow's teeth and gums, not any more than your toothbrush can do that for you. Have your Chow Chow's teeth cleaned at least once a year by your veterinarian (twice a year is better) and he will be happier, healthier, and far more pleasant to live with.

The Hercules™ by Nylabone® has been designed with strong jaws in mind. It is made of polyurethane, like car bumpers.

TRAINING

You owe proper training to your Chow Chow. The right and privilege of being trained is his birthright; and whether your Chow Chow is going to be a handsome, well-mannered housedog and companion, a show dog, or whatever possible use he may be put to, the basic training is always the same—all must start with basic obedience, or what might be called "manner training."

Your Chow Chow must come instantly when called and obey the "Sit" or "Down" command just as fast; he must walk quietly at "Heel," whether on or off lead. He must be mannerly and polite wherever he goes; he must be polite to strangers on the street and in stores. He must be mannerly in the presence of other dogs. He

Whether you are training your Chow Chow as a show dog or a house pet or both, acclimating him to wearing a leash and a collar is a must.

must not bark at children on roller skates, motorcycles, or other domestic animals. And he must be restrained from chasing cats. It is not a dog's inalienable right to chase cats, and he must be reprimanded for it.

PROFESSIONAL TRAINING

How do you go about this training? Well, it's a very simple procedure, pretty well standardized by now. First, if you can afford the extra expense, you may send your Chow Chow to a professional trainer, where in 30 to 60 days he will learn how to be a "good dog." If you enlist the services of a good professional trainer, follow his advice of when to come to see the dog. No, he won't forget you, but too-frequent visits at the wrong time may slow down his training progress. And using a "pro" trainer means that you will have to go for some training, too, after the trainer feels your Chow Chow is ready to go home. You will have to learn how your Chow Chow works, just what to expect of him and how to use what the dog has learned after he is home.

OBEDIENCE TRAINING CLASS

Another way to train your Chow Chow (many experienced Chow Chow people think this is the best) is to join an obedience training class right in your own community. There is such a group in nearly every community nowadays. Here you will be working with a group of people who are also just starting out. You will actually be training your own dog, since all work is done under the direction of a head trainer who will make suggestions

Obedience commands such as "stay" and "down" will ensure a well-mannered Chow Chow, both indoors and out.

to you and also tell you when and how to correct your Chow Chow's errors. Then, too, working with such a group, your Chow Chow will learn to get along with other dogs. And, what is more important, he will learn to do exactly what he is told to do, no matter how much confusion there is around him or how great the temptation is to go his own way.

Write to your national kennel club for the location of a training club or class in your locality. Sign up. Go to it regularly—every session! Go early and leave late! Both you and your Chow Chow will benefit tremendously.

TRAIN HIM BY THE BOOK

The third way of training your Chow Chow is by the book. Yes, you can do it this way and do a good job of it too. But in using the book method, select a book,

Successful Dog Training is one of the better dog training books. It is written by Michael Kamer, who trains dogs for movie stars.

Training classes provide an opportunity for your Chow Chow to learn to get along with other dogs as well as to obey commands despite distractions.

buy it, study it carefully; then study it some more, until the procedures are almost second nature to you. Then start your training. But stay with the book and its advice and exercises. Don't start in and then make up a few rules of your own. If you don't follow the book, you'll get into jams you can't get out of by yourself. If after a few hours of short training sessions your Chow Chow is still not working as he should, get back to the book for a study session, because it's your fault, not the dog's! The procedures of dog training have been so well systemized that it must be your fault, since literally thousands of fine Chow Chows have been trained by the book.

After your Chow Chow is "letter perfect" under all conditions, then, if you wish, go on to advanced training and trick work.

Your Chow Chow will love his obedience training, and you'll burst with pride at the finished product! Your Chow Chow will enjoy life even more, and you'll enjoy your Chow Chow more. And remember—you *owe good training to your Chow Chow.*

SHOWING YOUR CHOW CHOW

A show Chow Chow is a comparatively rare thing. He is one out of several litters of puppies. He happens to be born with a degree of physical perfection that closely approximates the standard by which the breed is judged in the show ring. Such a dog should, on maturity, be able to win or approach his championship in good, fast company at the larger shows. Upon finishing his championship, he is apt to be as highly desirable as a breeding animal. As a proven stud, he will automatically command a high price for service.

1994 Westminster Kennel Club Best of Breed winner Ch. Sunburst's Rocket Man owned by Hiroshi Matsumo. Westminster is the most prestigious dog show in the United States.

Showing Chow Chows is a lot of fun—yes, but it is a highly competitive sport. While all the experts were once beginners, the odds are against a novice. You will be showing against experienced handlers, often people who have devoted a lifetime to breeding, picking the right ones, and then showing those dogs through to their championships. Moreover, the most perfect Chow Chow ever born has faults, and in your hands the faults will be far more evident than with the experienced handler who knows how to minimize his Chow Chow's faults. These are but a few points on the sad side of the picture.

The experienced handler, as I say, was not born knowing the ropes. He learned—*and so can you!* You can if you will put in the same time, study and keen observation that he did. But it will take time!

KEY TO SUCCESS

First, search for a truly fine show prospect. Take the puppy home, raise him by the book, and as carefully as you know how, give him every chance to mature into the Chow Chow you hoped for. My advice is to keep your dog out of big shows, even Puppy Classes, until he is mature. Maturity in the male is roughly two years; with the female, 14 months or so. When your Chow Chow is approaching maturity, start out at match shows, and, with this experience for both of you, then

This beautiful Chow Chow won Best In Show at a dog show in Russia. Best In Show is the highest award at a dog show.

go gunning for the big wins at the big shows.

Next step, read the standard by which the Chow Chow is judged. Study it until you know it by heart. Having done this, and while your puppy is at home (where he should be) growing into a normal, healthy Chow Chow, go to every dog show you can possibly reach. Sit at the ringside and watch Chow Chow judging. Keep your ears and eyes open. Do your own judging, holding each of those dogs against the standard, which you now know by heart.

In your evaluations, don't start looking for faults. Look for the virtues—the best qualities. How does a given Chow Chow shape up against the standard? Having looked for and noted the virtues, then note the faults and see what prevents a given Chow Chow from standing correctly or moving well. Weigh these faults against the virtues, since, ideally, every feature of the dog should contribute to the harmonious whole dog.

When you bring your Chow Chow to a show, make sure you have the proper accommodations. A wire crate such as this one provides comfortable housing while the dog awaits his turn in the ring.

"RINGSIDE JUDGING"

It's a good practice to make notes on each Chow Chow, always holding the dog against the standard. In "ringside judging," forget your personal preference for this or that feature. What does the standard say about it? Watch carefully as the judge places the dogs in a given class. It is difficult from the ringside always to see why number one was placed over the second dog. Try to follow the judge's reasoning. Later try to talk with the judge after he is finished. Ask him questions as to why he placed certain Chow Chows and not others. Listen while the judge explains his placings, and, I'll say right here, any judge worthy of his license should be able to give reasons.

When you're not at the ringside, talk with the fanciers and breeders who have Chow Chows. Don't be afraid to ask opinions or say that you don't know. You have a lot of listening to do, and it will help you a great deal and speed up your personal progress if you are a good listener.

BELONGING TO A SPECIALTY CLUB

In all parts of the world where Chow Chows are popularly known there are specialty clubs devoted to the breed. Membership in these clubs is a very rewarding and constructive association for all, even for the most novice owners.

In the United States, the Chow Chow Club of America is the parent club, and is the American Kennel Club member specialty club for the breed. This specialty club in your immediate area; if so, ask that your name be proposed for membership. Dues in specialty clubs are usually quite nominal. There are many advantages in specialty club membership. Most of them conduct programs which include guest speakers at meetings,

Showing your Chow will be hard work for both you and your dog, but in the end it is worth it!

organization holds an annual specialty show, on a rotating basis, in various parts of the country, with the annual meeting being held in conjunction with the annual specialty show (usually taking place during the spring).

In addition to the parent club, there are numerous regional specialty clubs, each covering a specified area. When you purchase your Chow, be sure to discuss with the breeder whether or not there is a Chow Chow symposiums on the breed, training classes for show competition and obedience grooming classes, match shows, and a great deal more, not to mention the opportunity of making friends with *other* Chow owners.

The American Kennel Club, 51 Madison Avenue, New York, NY 10010, will provide you with the name and address of the Secretary of the Chow Chow Club, who can answer questions

After judging, the author poses with her choice for Group 1. Chow Chows are exhibited in the Non-Sporting Group in the United States and in the Utility Group in England.

regarding the parent club, or the location of and whom to contact for membership applications for the regional clubs.

ENTER MATCH SHOWS

With the ring deportment you have watched at big shows firmly in mind and practice, enter your Chow Chow in as many match shows as you can. When in the ring, you have two jobs. One is to see to it that your Chow Chow is always being seen to its best advantage. The other job is to keep your eye on the judge to see what he may want you to do next. Watch only the judge and your Chow Chow. Be quick and be alert; do exactly as the judge directs. Don't speak to him except to answer his questions. If he does something you don't like, don't say so. And don't irritate the judge (and everybody else) by constantly talking and fussing with your dog.

In moving about the ring, remember to keep clear of dogs beside you or in front of you. It is my advice to you *not* to show your Chow Chow in a regular point show until he is at least close to maturity and after both you and your dog have had time to perfect ring manners and poise in the match shows.

YOUR CHOW CHOW'S HEALTH

We know our pets, their moods and habits, and therefore we can recognize when our Chow Chow is experiencing an off-day. Signs of sickness can be very obvious or very subtle. As any mother can attest, diagnosing and treating an ailment require common sense, knowing when to seek home remedies and when to visit your doctor...or veterinarian, as the case may be.

Your veterinarian, we know, is your Chow Chow's best friend, next to you. It will pay to be choosy about your veterinarian. Talk to dog-owning friends whom you respect. Visit more than one vet before you make a lifelong choice. Trust your instincts. Find a knowledgeable, compassionate vet who knows Chow Chows and likes them.

Grooming for good health makes good sense. The rough Chow's coat is abundant, double and straight: of the two Chow coats it requires more brushing to keep mat-free and looking its best. With both types, brushing stimulates the natural oils in the coat and also removes dead haircoat. Chows shed seasonally, which means their undercoat (the soft downy white fur) is pushed out by the incoming new coat. A medium-strength bristle brush is all that is required to groom this beautiful breed of dog.

From puppy to adult, you should maintain your Chow Chow's health through regular veterinary visits.

Skin problems may arise from soap left in the Chow's coat, as well as from fleas and allergies. An owner's best effort to keep the Chow's coat immaculate and well groomed will pay off a hundredfold.

Anal sacs, sometimes called anal glands, are located in the musculature of the anal ring, one on either side. Each empties into the rectum via a small duct. Occasionally their secretion becomes thickened and accumulates so you can readily feel these structures from the outside. If your Chow Chow is scooting across the floor dragging his rear quarters, or licking his rear, his anal sacs may need to be

Chow Chow puppies are adorable and vulnerable, making inoculations a number-one priority. Your veterinarian will let you know the proper vaccination schedule for your new puppy.

expressed. Placing pressure in and up towards the anus, while holding the tail, is the general routine. Anal sac secretions are characteristically foul-smelling, and you could get squirted if not careful. Veterinarians can take care of this during regular visits and demonstrate the cleanest method.

Many Chow Chows are predisposed to certain congenital and inherited abnormalities, such as hip dysplasia, a blatantly common problem in purebred dogs with few exceptions. Unfortunately, the Chow Chow suffers from a high percentage rate of hip dysplasia despite the efforts of many conscientious breeders. This is due to the breed's unique straight stifles. New owners must insist on screening certificates from such hip registries as OFA or PennHIP. Since HD is hereditary, it's necessary to know that the parents and grandparents of your puppy had hips rated good or better. Dysplastic dogs suffer from badly constructed hip joints which become arthritic and very painful, thereby hindering the dog's ability to be a working dog, a good-moving show dog, or even a happy, active pet.

Chow Chows also suffer from elbow dysplasia, owing to their stifle construction, and the OFA screens for elbows as well. Young dogs typically show signs of limping or rotating elbows when walking or running, which may indicate that elbow dysplasia is present.

Osteochondritis dissecans affects the bone of many large breeds, and although many other breeds are more prone to this disease, the Chow Chow has been a victim on many occasions. Eye conditions such as glaucoma, cataracts, ectropion and entropion have become concerns for Chow breeders. Screening for eye problems has therefore been prioritized. Bilateral cataracts are the most frequently seen in Chow Chows, and can reduce a dog's vision. Entropion and ectropion, both affecting the eyelids, affect Chows. Although these can be corrected through surgery, they eliminate the dog from competing in dog shows as well as from breeding programs.

Hypothyroidism (malfunction of the thyroid gland) can be linked to many symptoms in Chows, such as obesity, lethargy, and reproductive disorders. Supplementation of the thyroid decreases problems, though such dogs should likely not be bred.

Breeders advise against feeding the Chow Chow one large meal per day because of the dangers of bloat (gastric torsion), the twisting of the stomach causes gas to build up and the organ expands like a balloon. Avoiding strenuous exercise and large amounts of water can preclude the occurrence of bloat, as can feeding two smaller meals instead of one larger one. A good commercial dog food is recommended for the dog's balanced diet.

Owners must also be aware that Chows are prone to heat stroke and cannot tolerate overexposure to the sun. Heat stroke can occur very quickly, especially with heavily coated dogs whose natural resistance to the sun is minimal. Guard against obesity, as overweight dogs have even less tolerance to the sun.

basic vaccinations to protect your dog are: parvovirus, distemper, hepatitis, leptospirosis, adenovirus, parainfluenza, coronavirus, bordetella, tracheobronchitis (kennel cough), Lyme disease and rabies.

Because of the Chow Chow's unique straight stifles, the breed suffers from a high percentage rate of hip dysplasia. New owners must insist on screening certificates from such hip registries as OFA or PennHIP, as this problem is hereditary.

For the continued health of your dog, owners must attend to vaccinations regularly. Your veterinarian can recommend a vaccination schedule appropriate for your dog, taking into consideration the factors of climate and geography. The

Parvovirus is a highly contagious, dog-specific disease, first recognized in 1978. Targeting the small intestine, parvo affects the stomach, and diarrhea and vomiting (with blood) are clinical signs. Although the dog can pass the infection to other dogs within three days of infection, the initial signs, which include lethargy and depression, don't display themselves until four to seven days. When affecting puppies under four weeks of age, the heart muscle is frequently attacked. When the heart is affected, the puppies exhibit difficulty in breathing and experience crying and foaming at the nose and mouth.

Distemper, related to human measles, is an airborne virus that spreads in the blood and ultimately in the nervous system and epithelial tissues. Young dogs or dogs with weak immune systems can develop encephalomyelitis (brain disease) from the distemper infection. Such dogs experience seizures, general weakness and rigidity, as well as "hardpad." Since distemper is largely incurable, prevention through vaccination is vitally important. Puppies should be vaccinated at six to eight weeks of age, with boosters at ten to 12 weeks. Older puppies (16 weeks and older) who are unvaccinated should receive no fewer than two vaccinations at three- to four-week intervals.

Hepatitis mainly affects the liver and is caused by canine adenovirus type I. Highly infectious, hepatitis often affects dogs nine to 12 months of age. Initially the virus localizes in the dog's tonsils and then disperses to the liver, kidneys and eyes. Generally speaking the dog's immune system is capable of combating this virus. Canine infectious hepatitis affects dogs whose systems cannot fight off the adenovirus. Affected dogs have fever, abdominal pains, bruising on mucous membranes and gums, and experience coma and convulsions. Prevention of hepatitis exists only through vaccination at eight to ten weeks of age and then boosters three or four weeks later, then annually.

Leptospirosis is a bacterium-related disease, often spread by rodents. The organisms that spread leptospirosis enter through the mucous membranes and spread to the internal organs via the bloodstream. It can be passed through the dog's urine. Leptospirosis does not affect young dogs as consistently as the other viruses; it is reportedly regional in distribution and somewhat dependent on the immunostatus of the dog. Fever, inappetence, vomiting, dehydration, hemorrhage, kidney and eye disease can result in moderate cases.

Bordetella, called canine cough, causes a persistent hacking cough in dogs and is very contagious. Bordetella involves a virus and a bacteria: parainfluenza is the most common virus implicated; Bordetella bronchiseptica, the bacterium. Bronchitis and pneumonia result in less than 20 percent of the cases, and most dogs recover from the condition within a week to four weeks. Non-prescription medicines can help relieve the hacking cough, though nothing

Good health begins on the outside. With plenty of exercise, proper nutrition, and good grooming, your Chow Chow will live a long, healthy life.

can cure the condition before it's run its course. Vaccination cannot guarantee protection from canine cough, but it does ward off the most common virus responsible for the condition.

Lyme disease (also called borreliosis), although known for decades, was only first diagnosed in dogs in 1984. Lyme disease can affect cats, cattle, and horses, but especially people. In the U.S., the disease is transmitted by two ticks carrying the *Borrelia burgdorferi* organism: the deer tick (*Ixodes scapularis*) and the western black-legged tick (*Ixodes pacificus*), the latter primarily affects reptiles. In Europe, *Ixodes ricinus* is responsible for spreading Lyme. The disease causes lameness, fever, joint swelling, inappetence, and lethargy. Removal of ticks from the dog's coat can help reduce the chances of Lyme, though not as much as avoiding heavily wooded areas where the dog is most likely to contract ticks. A vaccination is available, though it has not been proven to protect dogs from all strains of the organism that cause the disease.

Rabies is passed to dogs and people through wildlife: in North America, principally through the skunk, fox and raccoon; the bat is not the culprit it was once thought to be. Likewise, the common image of the rabid dog foaming at the mouth with every hair on end is unlikely the truest scenario. A rabid dog exhibits difficulty eating, salivates much and has spells of paralysis and awkwardness. Before a dog reaches this final state, it may experience anxiety, personality changes, irritability and more aggressiveness than is usual. Vaccinations are strongly recommended as rabid dogs are too dangerous to manage and are commonly euthanized. Puppies are generally vaccinated at 12 weeks of age, and then annually. Although rabies is on the decline in the world community, tens of thousands of humans die each year from rabies-related incidents.

Parasites have clung to our pets for centuries. Despite our modern efforts, fleas still pester our pet's existence, and our own. All dogs itch, and fleas can make even the happiest dog a miserable, scabby mess. The loss of hair and habitual biting and chewing at themselves rank among the annoyances; the nuisances include the passing of tapeworms and the whole family's itching through the summer months. A full range of flea-control and elimination products are available at pet shops, and your veterinarian surely has recommendations. Sprays, powders, collars and dips fight fleas from the outside; drops and pills fight the good fight from inside. Discuss the possibilities with your vet. Not all products can be used in conjunction with one another, and some dogs may be more sensitive to certain applications than others. The dog's living quarters must be debugged as well as the dog itself. Heavy infestation may require multiple treatments.

Always check your dog for ticks carefully. Although fleas can be acquired almost anywhere, ticks are more likely to be picked up in heavily treed areas, pastures or other outside grounds (such as dog shows or obedience or field trials). Athletic, active, and hunting dogs are the most likely subjects, though any passing dog can be the host. Remember Lyme disease is passed by tick infestation.

As for internal parasites, worms are potentially dangerous for dogs and people. Roundworms, hookworms, whipworms, tapeworms, and heartworms comprise the blightsome party of troublemakers. Deworming puppies begins at around two to three weeks and continues until three months of age. Proper hygienic care of the environment is also important to prevent contamination with roundworm and hookworm eggs. Heartworm preventatives are recommended by most veterinarians, although there are some drawbacks to the regular introduction of poisons into our dogs' systems. These daily or monthly preparations also help regulate most other worms as well. Discuss worming procedures with your veterinarian.

Roundworms pose a great threat to dogs and people. They are found in the intestines of dogs, and can be passed to people through ingestion of feces-contaminated dirt. Roundworm infection can be prevented by not walking dogs in heavy-traffic people areas, by burning feces, and by curbing dogs in a responsible manner. (Of course, in most areas of the country, curbing dogs is the law.) Roundworms are typically passed from the bitch to the litter, and the bitch should be treated along with the puppies, even if she tested negative prior to whelping. Generally puppies are treated every two weeks until two months of age.

Hookworms, like roundworms, are also a danger to dogs and

This Chow Chow shows off his characteristic blue/black tongue. The Chow and the Chinese Shar-Pei are the only two breeds of dog to have this distinctive feature.

people. The hookworm parasite (known as *Ancylostoma caninum*) causes cutaneous larva migrans in people. The eggs of hookworms are passed in feces and become infective in shady, sandy areas. The larvae penetrate the skin of the dog, and the dog subsequently becomes infected. When swallowed, these parasites affect the intestines, lungs, windpipe, and the whole digestive system. Infected dogs suffer from anemia and lose large amounts of blood in the places where the worms latch onto the dog's intestines, etc.

Although infrequently passed to humans, whipworms are cited as one of the most common parasites in America. These elongated worms affect the intestines of the dog, where they latch on, and cause colic upset or diarrhea. Unless identified in stools passed, whipworms are difficult to diagnose. Adult worms can be eliminated more consistently than the larvae, since whipworms exhibit unusual life cycles. Proper hygienic care of outdoor grounds is critical to the avoidance of these harmful parasites.

Tapeworms are carried by fleas, and enter the dog when the dog swallows the flea. Humans can acquire tapeworms in the same way, though we are less likely to swallow fleas than dogs are. Recent studies have shown that certain rodents and other wild animals have been infected with tapeworms, and dogs can be affected by catching and/or eating these other animals. Of course, outdoor hunting dogs and terriers are more likely to be infected in this way than are your typical housedog or non-motivated hound. Treatment for tapeworm has proven very effective, and infected dogs do not show great discomfort or symptoms. When people are infected, however, the liver can be seriously damaged. Proper cleanliness is the best bet against tapeworms.

Heartworm disease is transmitted by mosquitoes and badly affects the lungs, heart and blood vessels of dogs. The larvae of *Dirofilaria immitis* enters the dog's bloodstream when bitten by an infected mosquito. The larvae takes about six months to mature. Infected dogs suffer from weight loss, appetite loss, chronic coughing and general fatigue. Not all affected dogs show signs of illness right away, and carrier dogs may be affected for years before clinical signs appear. Treatment of heartworm disease has been effective but can be dangerous also. Prevention as always is the desirable alternative. Ivermectin is the active ingredient in most heartworm preventatives and has proven to be successful. Check with your veterinarian for the preparation best for your dog. Dogs generally begin taking the preventatives at eight months of age and continue to do so throughout the non-winter months.